On Connection

Further praise for *On Connection*:

'*On Connection* is soul work, deeply felt and beautifully wrought. The truth-speaker Kae Tempest takes to non-fiction with grace, musicality and innate essayistic skill. The book glows with their trademark honesty and questing integrity.'

MAX PORTER

'I identify with [*On Connection*] so deeply . . . I love it.'

FLEA

'A powerful and digestible essay on the power of creativity and connection . . . everyone should read this right now, especially makers & creators looking for hope in 2020's existential burn.'

GEMMA CAIRNEY

'Kae Tempest has added one more string to an already crowded bow . . . [their thoughts] are surely worth repeating in this disconnected, distracted world. Tempest, as you'd expect, delivers them gorgeously, rhythmically, but also with clarity and a fierce grace. I drank *On Connection* down like a fresh glass of water.'

HOLLY WILLIAMS, *OBSERVER*

'Tempest's prose is crisp and thoughtful, and they are as willing to own up to their own mistakes and flaws as they are eager to insist upon the importance of the arts as a resource for cultivating greater self-awareness.'

NEW STATESMAN

'This finely crafted, deeply thoughtful essay examines creativity as an electrical current that connects the atomised individual with the larger whole . . . With searing honesty about personal struggles and failings, Tempest cuts through the ego-driven aspects of artistic creation.'

SYDNEY MORNING HERALD

'With its emphasis on empathy and the importance of being present, this slender book, which will appeal mostly to readers with an interest in mindfulness, is a welcome tonic to the fractured dissonance of modern life. A lyrical, tender linguistic balm.'

KIRKUS

'[An] eloquent work composed during the 2020 pandemic lockdown . . . elegant and well-turned. This thoughtful meditation will resonate with anyone looking for new ways to engage with their creativity.'

PUBLISHERS WEEKLY

Kae Tempest

On Connection

faber

First published in the UK and the USA in 2020
by Faber & Faber Limited
The Bindery, 51 Hatton Garden
London EC1N 8HN

This paperback edition first published in 2022

Typeset by Faber & Faber Limited
Printed and bound by CPI Group (UK) Ltd, Croydon, CR0 4YY

Extract from 'the creative act' from *The Last Night of the Earth Poems* by Charles
Bukowski. Copyright © 1992 by the Estate of Charles Bukowski. Courtesy of ECCO,
an imprint of HarperCollins Publishers.

Extract from 'Gathering Apricots' in *Provinces: Poems 1987–1991* by Czesław Miłosz;
English translation by Robert Hass. Copyright © 1991 by Czesław Miłosz Royalties,
Inc. Courtesy of ECCO, an imprint of HarperCollins Publishers (US) and from *New
and Collected Poems 1931–2001* by © Czesław Miłosz 1988, 1991, 1995, 2001. Published
by HarperCollins 2001, Allen Lane, The Penguin Press 2001, Penguin Classics 2005.
Reproduced by permission of Penguin Books Ltd. (UK)

Extracts from *Kabir: Ecstatic Poems*, translated by Robert Bly
(Boston: Beacon Press, 2004).

Extract from 'Lie, Cheat, Steal' by Killer Mike and El-P (Run the Jewels), from *Run the
Jewels 2* [digital release], (New York: Mass Appeal, 2014).

A CIP record for this book
is available from the British Library

ISBN 978-0-571-37043-6

MIX
Paper | Supporting
responsible forestry
FSC® C171272
www.fsc.org

Printed and bound in the UK on FSC® certified paper in line with our continuing
commitment to ethical business practices, sustainability and the environment.
For further information see faber.co.uk/environmental-policy

For Assia Ghendir

Unknown, not unperceived

WILLIAM BLAKE

Running Order

Set Up

Dip him in the river who loves water.

WILLIAM BLAKE

This is a book about connection. About how immersion in creativity can bring us closer to each other and help us cultivate greater self-awareness. About how fine-tuning the ability to feel a creative connection can help us develop our empathy and establish a deeper relationship between ourselves and the world.

I understand that even calling for connection and universality is problematic in a time of such division. Whether it's Black Lives Matter or All Lives Matter, trans rights or terf rights, anti-vax or vaccinate, this is a time to take sides. And the stakes are high. Calling for togetherness risks minimising the necessity of people fighting for basic rights and freedoms. There are good reasons for the canyons that have opened up between us.

I do not believe that 'our differences don't matter' or that we are all the same. I acknowledge the social,

3

historical, economic and political context of our differences and how they impact upon our lives. I also think that beneath our direct lived experiences and our inherited or ancestral experiences – beneath our unique cultures and identities – there is commonality, and I believe that this is something we can all access through creativity.

Creativity encourages connection. And connection to true, uncomfortable self allows us to take responsibility for our impact on other people, rather than going blindly through life in a disconnected buzz of one day into the next, taking what we can from every encounter with no further thought possible than *my survival, my kids' survival, my survival, my kids' survival.*

/

Over the course of the following chapters, I will write in praise of creativity, in praise of music and theatre, and in praise of gathering to feel together. I understand that what humans need, more than the opportunity to attend a concert or act in a play, is access to secure affordable housing, safe and fair working conditions, healthcare, readily available fresh, non-toxic food and water, and an environment for their families to grow up in that is not violent, dangerous or traumatic. But it is also my understanding that, right beside these basic requirements, humans have always needed – and will always need – to play, to create, to reflect and release.

I will use these terms to explore my ideas: creativity, connection and creative connection.

Creativity is the ability to feel wonder and the desire to respond to what we find startling. Or, more simply, creativity is any act of love. Any act of making. It is usually applied to art-making, but it can also be applied to anything you do that requires your focus, skill and ingenuity. It takes creativity to dress well, for example. To parent. To paint a windowsill. To give someone you love your full attention.

Connection is the feeling of landing in the present tense. Fully immersed in whatever occupies you, paying close attention to the details of experience. Characterised by an awareness of your minuteness in the scheme of things. A feeling of being absolutely located. Right here. Regardless of whether that 'right here' is agitated or calm, joyous or painful.

Creative connection is the use of creativity to access and feel connection and get yourself and those

5

with you in the moment into a more connected space.

It could be that connection to another, deeper world is most easily experienced by artists. But really, anyone who's ever meditated, prayed, studied the stars, cooked an important meal for people they love, thrown a punch, received one, built something with their hands, learned a skill because they had no choice, been in service to others, volunteered their time, found themselves at the edge of their sanity or at the edge of their experience, accepted a difficult truth, put themselves second, genuinely gone out of their way for somebody else, has felt it. Connection is not the sole domain of artists, but art is a good way of understanding the fruit of that other place where commonality begins.

When I refer to 'the reader', I may be referring to the person who engages with text, music or artworks, but I am also referring to the person engaging with friends, strangers, lovers and the world around them. The reader is the gate that has to open to let the meaning through.

When I refer to 'the writer', I may be referring to a writer of text or music, but also to the author of experience. The part of you that creates the narrative of your existence and that is constantly trying to find any thread strong enough to pull you through the blank pages of one day into the next.

/

James Joyce told me once: 'In the particular is contained the universal.' I appreciated the advice. It taught me that the closer attention I pay to my 'particular', the better chance I have of reaching you in yours.

I've been getting on the mic for twenty years now, desperate for every opportunity to speak and be heard. Along the way, I've walked into a lot of rooms and thought to myself, *Man, I don't know how it's going to happen tonight.* I've felt myself judged. Felt myself the wrong person for the occasion. I've looked out at crowds and judged them. Been faced with people who I know are not 'my people', and thought, *There's no way you and I are going to get there together.* And time and time again I've been proven wrong.

I have spent twenty years with a pen in my hand. Twenty years studying the art of words spoken in places to people. Everything I have seen, I have seen through the lens of my creativity; it has been the primary function of my life.

7

I will discuss writing, reading and performance here because it's what I know to be true. I will be referring to these things specifically, but by referring to them, I will also be referring to the bigger themes of who we are, how we live, and how we might open ourselves to others.

Empathy is remembering that everybody has a story. Multiple stories. And remembering to make space to hear someone else's story before immediately telling your own.

I love people so much. Every time I'm close to the edge, I am brought back into focus by paying deliberate attention to the people I encounter every day.

Yes, I write for others like me. Others who don't fit, have never fitted. Dykes like me. Who realise there's nothing to be gained from even trying to fit, and eventually have just had to find their own way through.

Others who give a shit about the world.

Others who see the beauty first and are driven to witness the carnage.

Others who see the carnage first and are driven to witness the beauty.

But also, for those who have always fitted.

For those who don't give a shit about anything.

For those who've never seen the beauty anywhere. And even less, the carnage. Just outline things and passing time.

People who share my beliefs and people who find them fucking ridiculous.

Everyone. All the time. No matter what.

Sound Check

The fox condemns the trap, not himself.

WILLIAM BLAKE

The problem with reflection is that before looking in the mirror, we compose ourselves. So what we see is what we hope to see. Before the furtive glance into the dark glass of a parked car or shop window, we have already made the face or taken the posture that we like to see. We adapt for the shock of observation. To really see ourselves requires a different approach.

To locate ourselves fully in the present is difficult. What do we stand for? How do we square our beliefs with the realities of our lives as consumers? You may feel like the good guy, sure. But how can you be certain? When was the last time you noticed yourself behaving in a way that conflicted with your beliefs? Does it not happen daily that you transgress your own codes? You may be sure that you stand for honesty and integrity, but you still lied to your partner and deleted the texts. You still lost your temper in the car and screamed at your son.

If we are to come to a better understanding of our behaviour, we need to know ourselves not only as we'd like to be, but in how we actually operate. Who do you perform as when you are with different groups of people? Would you let a racist or homophobic remark slide from an acquaintance because it would break your personal social code to interject and pull them up on it? If so, are you prepared to accept that you lack integrity? That social conformity means you hold your desire to please people or avoid confrontation in higher regard than your morals?

The twin existences of who we hope to be and who we actually are have been a longstanding literary obsession. We tell endless stories about the forces that compete for our souls, whether it's Faust and his devils, Kendrick Lamar's K. Dot trying to find his way through in *good kid, m.A.A.d city*, or Odysseus blessed by Pallas Athena and punished by Poseidon. These works encourage close examination of motives and morals. But it's much easier to surrender responsibility to gods or circumstance than take matters into our own hands and say, *Perhaps I am not who I consider myself to be. Perhaps, in truth, I have never really considered myself at all.*

We have grown far from ourselves. The charades we are expected to perform have become real and swallowed us into the act. How else could we cope with the parameters of our lives? If not by virtue of the chips we stack to prove ourselves worthwhile. If not by believing in the farce.

And we have grown far from each other.

/

Numbness, or disconnection, is a lack of true feeling. Maintaining a surface engagement with whatever is going on while at the same time being entirely elsewhere. So consumed with the concerns of the day, the actual events of the day pass unnoticed or are so unbearably precise they are experienced in the hyper-real close-up of a perceived threat to your life.

Feel that heaviness mounting behind every action? The depravity of the desire to remain calm and not give in? Are you the type to hold yourself to irrational account? Listen without listening? Taste without tasting? Do you suppress rather than face conflict? Feel that everything is somehow a pretence? Are you going through the motions without truly landing on anything? Unable to notice your own preferences or feelings, let alone make them priorities? Are you uninterested in anything that taxes the inner reserves?

What inner reserves?

Who is the offstage self? The non-public you? The you that you are when your partner, parent, children, friends are not around? The you that doesn't go to work or pay the bills? The you that hasn't dropped out, isn't smoking crack, hasn't found themselves without a place to live? The you that isn't proud of doing well at work? The you that isn't soothed by a new relationship, a new haircut, a new pair of shoes or a new storage solution? The you whose morality is not informed by the newspapers you read or the politics you ascribe to? The you that you encounter in the middle of the night, waking from a dream, sure you heard a noise outside the door?

The same 'you' that's in everyone else.

/

Numbness is a logical response to the onslaught of the age. In order to be able to survive it with any semblance of sanity, in order to be able to function or even to flourish, numbness is required. A numbness that is evident when commuting in rush hour, or walking through a busy shopping district or a recently gentrified neighbourhood, or kissing your partner while thinking of something else. Doing the numbing chores of a life at the end of a numbing day of doing whatever it is that you do to sustain your existence. The precarious numbness of drunkenness, of unfeeling sexual encounters, of cheap drugs or expensive drugs. A numbness that is permissive, distractive, that rewards itself with deeper and deeper numbness. The numbness of leaving the body and leaving the mind and leaving the room saying, 'Life goes on.' 'It is what it is.' 'Get over yourself.' 'Got to keep moving.' 'Got to get it done.' Getting things done, always getting things done, in a permanent state of mild or severe disassociation. Binge watch. Binge drink. Binge eat. Oblivion.

I know this numbness because it is my life.

I have sought numbness. Over many years I have thrown myself fully into the pursuit of getting numb. Losing feeling. Avoiding instead of arriving in my experiences. I have needed something all-consuming to snap me out of reality. I have chosen to use drugs and alcohol to get me away from the pressures of my brain and the world. This has been both positive and negative. Numbness can be beautiful. It can be necessary. We need balance. When a life slips too far into disconnection or too far into connection, it is an exhausting process, trying to reanimate the avatar or re-root the uprooted.

I find myself looking for the antidote to numbness. But there is no need to vaccinate against it or to banish it from the palette of experience. Numbness is part of experience.

This, as ever, is my privilege talking. To be in a position of being able to ignore the reality of what this system does and continues to do is to be wholly complicit in it. Is to benefit hugely from it. To be able to not think about how the winners in this game came by their vast stores of mineral wealth is to profit from that wealth. The long list of ransacked nations, installed dictators, insurgencies financed by corporate interests, jailed bodies, ruined land. Death, disease and pipelines. To be able to ignore the inequality in your own city is to prosper from that inequality. The criminalisation of black bodies by an institutionally racist state. The rising use of food banks. The families still living in temporary accommodation years after the horror of Grenfell.

Don't think, I don't want to think. I'm stuck in my habits and nothing is real but the utter expanse and I can't move and I can't stop moving. They've pulled all my shifts now I can't make the rent and I'm still waiting for the council to get back to my enquiries and I'm getting by on help from my friends but it won't last for ever. I can't feel anything. I'm a good person. I spend time talking to heartbroken friends, I offer them all my best careful advice. I do what I can for my family, I'm always visiting. I don't make inappropriate jokes, the children all like me. I get on with animals. I remember to flirt with my husband. I buy my wife jewellery for Christmas. I can't feel anything.

James Baldwin captures the immersion of obsessive love in *Giovanni's Room*: 'Life in that room seemed to be occurring beneath the sea, time flowed past indifferently above us, hours and days had no meaning' We have found ourselves in a similar swamp of unreachability, of timelessness and delay. It is like being lost in a toxic pairing. I know I don't want it. But I don't know how to get out.

This system needs your numbness. You are an agent of consumption. You have no other purpose in the eyes of your government. You are nothing. Grease for a machine that relies on your complicity and your passionate malleability. You have been led to believe you are the kernel of a bright, bright future, and that all you have to do to live your best life is compete. Win. Consume. You are a consumer and your parents were consumers and your grandparents were consumers and your children are consumers. This is your legacy. Since the Enlightenment, that hallowed age of European bloodlust, which has peddled its own importance and propagated its own mythology in our schools and textbooks and on our television screens as the age of unmatched artistic and philosophical excellence, the age of fraternity and libertarianism when in truth it was an age of violence, civil and global war, inequality, repression and savage cruelty. Running on blood. The blood of the working classes. The blood of the black and brown bodies exploited and sold and killed for its progress. Bloodied and shameful and standing on columns in all of our terrible cities, proud stone temples to an age of evil that sold itself as the Age of Light. We live in that time still. Its chaos, ongoing. The industrialisation of inequality continues. Your numbness is necessary. My numbness is necessary.

And yet.

Telling poems levels the room.

I've seen it happen, so many times, in so many different environments. Because there's no music, no set, no backdrop, no need for anything other than a person speaking and a person listening, a 'spoken-word' performance can happen anywhere, and as poets, when we get booked, we turn up, no matter how random it seems. I've told poems in art galleries in Central London, at queer parties in DIY spaces, to a group of young people in a homeless shelter, to the CEO of a global bank on a private mountain range, to an outlaw motorcycle gang at a shrimp shack on the Pacific Coast Highway. All with the same shaking hands, the same urgent desire to connect, and the same feeling that something drastic was about to change. I've gone on between punk bands at squat gigs, over jungle DJs in free parties, after awkward introductions in school classrooms and pupil referral units, in an opera house in an Italian village, in street-corner ciphers and at fundraising buffet functions for arts institutions. I got booked once for a poetry set in a mainstream comedy tent; the whole crowd waiting for a famous comedian and I shuffled out to talk about Icarus. I've told poems in libraries, in between circus acts in apocalyptic sci-fi festival zones, at cabaret side-show cocktail clubs, at rap battles, in people's living rooms, at a pub when the football was on, in the street outside someone else's gig, in the car park of the Albert Hall. Once I got booked to stand on the bar of a busy pub and just shout my poems and it seemed all right at the time. I've told poems in a sports shop for a fleet of runners back from a sprint; I was still in the clothes from the night before, with burst blood vessels in my face from all the drink I was putting away, telling poems with vaguely motivational themes while they cooled down in Lycra. I've told loads of poems in the foyers of venues. It seemed we were always going on in the foyer, giving everything we could to the passing crowd as they left the main gig in the auditorium and went to find the toilets or join the queue for rosé.

Naked language has a humanising effect; listening to someone tell their story, people noticeably opened up, became more vulnerable, and let their defences down; the rooms got less frosty, less confrontational. Once I told poems for the inmates at

HMP Holloway, and my words took on resonances they had *never* had before. Suddenly every single line was about the very moment of that performance and it was a powerful experience for me. Around the same time, I told poems at the opening of the Louis Vuitton Maison in Bond Street, and the same thing happened. The words took on a sharpness and resonance they had never had before. I was there, in my tracksuit bottoms, treading on the toes of supermodels, feeling completely exposed and judged, but I started to tell the poems, and the energy transformed, mine included; everybody opened up. Each time I have walked into strange rooms with poems to tell, I have had to confront my own insecurities and judgements about who I was talking to and why, and each time I was taught something about what connects us being more powerful than what divides.

Doors

Without Contraries is no progression.
WILLIAM BLAKE

In 1913, Carl Jung, a major figure in forming psycho-
therapy, psychiatry and psychology, began an eigh-
teen-year journey towards 'confronting the unconscious'. He developed a technique called 'active
imagination', which allowed him to pursue inner
images. He took himself to his study late at night
and embarked on gruelling sessions of writing and
painting, which sometimes left him in great distress,
approaching the edge of his sanity. What he discovered in those experiments formed the core of all his
later published works. He wrote of those years as
the 'numinous beginning, which contained everything'. He kept records of his nightly experiments,
and eventually wrote them up into what is known as
the *Red Book*. It remained unpublished until 2000,
thirty-nine years after his death.

In early 2016, I had just come off the back of
an eighteenth-month tour of my first solo album,

27

Everybody Down. It was a hardcore, no-frills tour which saw us go from playing Corsica Studios (a two hundred capacity venue) to the Electric Brixton (two thousand capacity). We travelled up and down the country and across the continent in the Welfare Unit, a second-hand van that had once been a 'comfort vehicle', parked up on motorways for the people working the roads. We ripped the toilet out the back to stash the instruments. It had eight seats, multiple hand-soap dispensers and an industrial tea urn. We were three weeks into a winter tour of Northern Europe before we worked out how to put the heating on. Somewhere in the middle of all this, I published my debut novel, *The Bricks that Built the Houses*, and so I found myself headed over to the States to launch it in cafes and book stores. A few nights into the US book tour, I was in Portland, Oregon, feeling drained and disoriented, passing time writing lyrics in a park near the venue.

I'd been rattled by the magnitude of street homelessness in the States, especially on the warmer West Coast. One guy I met in LA had a bed-frame, mattress and an armchair set up, even a bedside lamp with the plug ripped off. People I spoke to explained to me that street homelessness is closely linked with mental illness in the popular imagination, and it is in reality, too; a Harvard study places the figure of serious mental illness in the street homeless population at 30 per cent. This created a level of practical invisibility despite the very visible nature of establishing a home on the street where people walk every day. The people I spoke with – colleagues from the publishing world, other artists and also just people I met as I went about my day – all functioned under the general belief that homeless people were seriously mentally ill, and that all interactions should be avoided, in case of danger. I was staying in posh hotels in 'uptown' areas of the cities where there were large populations of street homeless. The parallel between the 'functioning' and 'non-functioning' members of society was so fucking stark. And the way these two factions of humanity existed without ever interacting seemed so carefully choreographed to me, an outsider, observing.

The way we have decided to live on this planet is sinister and strange.

I knew that in a couple of days, I would be leaving the States to fly to Australia, where I was due to give the opening address at the Sydney Writers' Festival. I was unsure of what I was going to say, and was turning ideas over in my mind, but the task felt beyond me.

I could see the impact of colonial bloodlust in everything I looked at. There was a deep violence at the core of things, and a screaming contrast between the built-up cities: the rampant shine of their capitalist success, and the feel from the land itself. A feeling bigger, deeper and more real than the neon and glass and the service-with-a-smile.

I was very tired. I felt lonely. And the world was a hypocrite, full of spite. I was thinking, *What use is writing? What can it really do?*

I got chatting with this guy that lived in the park. He saw me writing in my notebook and he came over, we greeted each other and started to talk. He was interested in what I was doing. I explained I was a poet from London. He loved poetry. He was in his early sixties, I would guess, but could have been older. He told me he'd had the same copy of this one particular book of poetry since he was seventeen. His mother had given it to him. It was a slim green paperback volume of Derek Walcott. Throughout all the experiences of his life, all the changes in circumstance, all the places he had lived and had to leave, he had kept this one book with him. He talked about how it made him feel human to have this book of poetry in his pocket, made him feel close to his mother and the child he had been and gave him great comfort. I was moved by the connection I made with that man. He was a very gentle person.

/

When I was asked to write this, the brief was: a work of non-fiction for a series of short pamphlets. I had the feeling that the publisher was hoping for something Political. But I decided to write what I know. I know creativity. I have been in a strange and passionate relationship with my own creativity since I was twelve or thirteen, suffering from mental health problems and using drugs and alcohol to cope with a difficult brain, troubles at home and gender dysphoria. I was a teenage runaway, a school drop-out and a drug dealer but white enough and middle class enough to have that not ruin my entire life or become the definition of me. These privileges afforded me the space to make mistakes. The same mistakes made by black and working-class friends of mine resulted in jail time, hospitalisation and, in a few cases, death.

Rest in peace Alfie my beautiful friend. And rest in peace Omar. I will not forget you.

At the time, I did not see it that way. I was lost. Sleeping in churchyards with my best mate and his heroin addiction, or allowing myself to get in a car with a fifty-year-old stranger who bought me beer and cigarettes because I let him touch me. Every day was just about trying to make enough money to get fucked up. That was the major goal of my life. I was in a lot of pain. Somehow, creativity reached through the fog when nothing else could. It gave me guidance, offered me purpose and connected me to all other creative people. It was transformative. I fell in love with music. I fell absolutely head over heels in love and I became joyful. I experienced creativity as my older self, or higher self: a voice that literally came into my head and told me what to do. I found community with the writers and musicians whose work I immersed myself in. I found a calling and pursued it with an obsessional fixation. It gave me new direction, new friendships and diverted me away from where I was heading, when I needed it the most. As I have grown, my creativity has been the constant that has grown with me. Always here. Always demanding I work harder to become the kind of person I want to be. Giving me the energy to pursue ideas in new ways. Keeping me alive.

Along the journey I have come up against a lot of people who just don't get it. In the past, I understood them as being 'closed' people, completely switched off. I used to get frustrated with these people, angry at a lack of 'consciousness'. If I could only 'reach' them, I was sure that I could 'change their minds'. But now, thankfully, I see things differently. I see that every single person is affected by the violence of existence in different ways, and that people carry their burdens however they can. People suffer a great deal, and ideally they must process their traumas in order to reach some kind of peace. But what if your situation is too intense and you can't get a moment's respite? People respond differently to things. People have different things to respond to. I am no one to judge how someone has come to a conclusion. I am no one to judge what conclusions someone has come to. I do not want to change minds any more. I just want to connect.

Why was it that this man was sleeping in the park while I was afforded the opportunities to travel the world with my poetry? It would be nice for me to believe I've earned every success with my hard work, my talent and my determination, but the truth is, the game is rigged. If I wasn't white and young-looking, and so coded as 'unthreatening', would I have really got away with saying half the things I've said over the years? Let alone been lauded for it? (In my earlier interviews the journalists *always* referred to my 'angelic' looks, my 'golden' hair, my baby face and my preoccupation with Greek mythology, constant references to which must have served to solidify my 'acceptability'.)

If things were different, if life was fair and presented all people with the same opportunities, would he not have been the poet on the international tour and me the one sleeping in the park?

Behind every exchange and encounter, every missed chance or lucky break, behind every event or non-event in a person's life, there are entire weather systems, pushing for or pushing against.

My gig that evening was in a bookstore called Powell's City of Books. It was a huge place, awe-inspiring. I looked around for a while, flying my hope like a battered old kite; *Are any of you people haunting the shelves writers like me? Want to kick it outside and smoke a cigarette?* But nope. Nothing.

I wandered upstairs to where the event was taking place; a few chairs lined up in front of a microphone. I noticed a small room the other side of the staircase, glass-panelled. The people inside stood still, heads bowed at the display cases. I read the inscription on the door: *Rare Book Room.* I asked an attendant if I could look around in there; she said, 'Sure, honey, go ahead.' I pushed open the door and walked into the hush of old words.

On a plinth in the centre of a glass display case, in between large photographic journals and leather-bound antiques, I saw Jung's *Red Book.* It was about a foot high, lit from beneath, and open at the first pages. I read those pages and felt my breathing change; something in the language was calling to me. I had been feeling so out of sorts and close to the edge. I didn't want to get up and do a reading in a bookstore and answer questions about my novel. I just wanted to sit in the park and talk to my friend until it was time to fly to the next place. But seeing that book and reading that page, I felt myself rediscovered.

Speak then of sick delusion when the spirit of the depths can no longer stay down and forces a man to speak in tongues instead of in human speech, and makes him believe that he himself is the spirit of the depths. But also speak of sick delusion when the spirit of this time does not leave a man and forces him to see only the surface, to deny the spirit of the depths and to take himself for the spirit of the times. The spirit of this time is ungodly, the spirit of the depths is ungodly, balance is godly.

I bought a copy of the reader's edition, a smaller, text-only version, and I sat down to read it on the empty chairs laid out for my event. I remember looking up, confused, at the smiling, pigeon-bodied man who tapped my elbow when people started drifting in to hear the talk.

That night, at my event, I spoke about creativity. About the narratives we construct that hold the world together and that pull the world apart. About the importance of literature and storytelling in cultivating deeper empathy and the importance of maintaining awareness of the rampant inequality of life in our system. I continued to think about these themes throughout that book tour, and in fact spoke about them in the opening address at the Sydney Writers'

Festival. All the things that I set out in this text, in fact, began to percolate in my mind back then, in that bookstore in Portland after meeting that man in the park and discovering Jung in the rare book room.

It's important to acknowledge that while I continued to travel the world and speak to the crowds who had gathered to hear, the substance of the things I was speaking about had been informed and inspired by an encounter with a man whose name I never knew, who does not have the opportunity in this text to speak for himself.

/

In the *Red Book*, Jung explores at length his idea that a person is governed by two spirits: the spirit of the times and the spirit of the depths. This idea chimed with me so resolutely that it became a crucial part of my understanding of the human condition.

In my reading of it, the spirit of the times is the part of you that is preoccupied with ordering your life into a narrative that you can stomach, the part of you that is concerned with current issues, current trends and the pursuits of the day. The part of you that urges you to achieve a particular set of goals, whether that's having children, finding a partner, giving up drink or drugs, or making enough money to leave your home town. The part of you that works towards something concrete. The part of you that cares about respectability or the approval of your peers.

The spirit of the depths is the ancient part of you. The part that responds to the invisible world. The part that makes no sense and speaks in heavy symbols. Your madness, your dreams, your visions. The spirit of the depths communicates through archetypes, masks, animal shapes. It is drawn to nature and wilderness. The spirit of the depths is not satisfied when you obtain the things the spirit of the times told you that you needed in order to live a satisfying life. The spirit of the depths sees the soul

as a living and self-existing being, and with this he contradicts the spirit of this time for whom the soul is a thing dependent on man, which lets himself be judged and arranged, and whose circumference we can grasp. I had to accept that what I had previously called my soul was not at all my soul, but a dead system.

In the *Red Book*, Jung searches for the spirit of the depths and the spirit of the times, actively pursues them, challenges them and invites them to speak through him. He induces in himself a kind of trance. He takes himself to the brink of psychosis to convene with spirits and visions in order that he may at last 'refind' his soul.

He whose desire turns away from outer things, reaches the place of the soul. If he does not find the soul, the horror of emptiness will overcome him, and fear will drive him with a whip lashing time and again in a desperate endeavour and a blind desire for the hollow things of the world. He becomes a fool through his endless desire, and forgets the way of his soul, never to find her again. He will run after all things, and will seize hold of them, but he will not find his soul, since he would find her only in himself.

We have been running after all things, we have been seizing hold of them, but we have not found our soul, since we would find it only in ourselves.

The internet seems to me to be the ultimate expression of the spirit of the times; it is the multi-voice of the collective conscious. But it cannot represent the collective subconscious; the spirit of the depths speaks through poetry and music, through fiction, image and myth. It is offline. Underneath. Reached through creative ritual and abandonment to something wild and in many ways terrifying.

For Jung, a person needs to maintain a strong inner balance between the spirit of the times and the spirit of the depths; too much of either creates neuroses. And as for the individual, so for society. Culturally, we have allowed the scales to shift dramatically; we are cut off from our deeper natures, we have turned our back on the spirit of the depths and live entirely in the spirit of the times. In order to regain our balance, we need to remaster the ability to go deep, to 'turn away from outer things'. To face what is in ourselves. This starts with connection and creativity.

Support Act

The most sublime act is to set another
before you.
WILLIAM BLAKE

Reading and re-reading the same passage ten times, the reader gives up on the book. They keep finding the text interrupted by their own thoughts. They read to access their own experience, to recall their past, consider their relationships or establish their own views more firmly. They are unable to read others without primarily reading themselves. They drop the book into their lap and go back to their phone.

Meanwhile, across town, a person is listening to music while they go about the business of clearing up their flat, ordering something from the internet and arranging a birthday drink with a group of friends. Multiple distractions need their attention and the music is an aide to staying focused on these other things. They listen to a playlist organised by an algorithm and only notice what's playing when they realise they don't like a song and have to skip it. Later, they work out in their bedroom to an upbeat gym playlist, and then they spend the evening studying at the kitchen table to a generic piano playlist. Any composer, any year, any player. Just select *chill piano for concentration*. Music for mood. Everything's yours. Take what you want. Get what you can.

In an upstairs classroom a student is learning to read without their creative energies roused, to better prepare them for life in the workplace; they are taught not to respond energetically to text but instead to remain distant, to take from rather than be a part of the experience. They annotate, discuss, question, abstract the meaning in order to better get a sense of the context.

/

The tendencies of our time are stamped so violently upon us, they emerge in our actions unbidden.

When we are fixated on what we can get from an exchange, or how we can benefit, instead of considering what we can offer, we are being exploitative. This fixation can be so intrinsic, we imagine ourselves innocent of it. Unintentional exploitation is exploitation, none the less.

A sign of the times: our consumptive, atomised

lives are framed by the proud narrative that civilisation evolved from an aggressive instinct; our kill-or-be-killed mentality got us here, from cave-dwellers to sky-scrapers. Man the hunter. Man the war-maker. Man the coloniser. Man the democratic consumer. Competition is natural. Competition breeds progress.

But is human nature separatism, tribalism and passionate distrust of the 'other'? Or is it co-operation, recognition and, provided basic needs are met, a live-and-let-live attitude to all? What's your own nature? How do you know? Is it what you tell yourself it is, or is it better observed in the things you find yourself doing that you wish you hadn't done? What is the nature of the people you share your life with? How closely do you even notice your own behaviour? Not your own *feelings*, but your own actions? How closely do you notice the behaviour of others?

What if we came to civilisation not from our capacities as hunters, but from our capacities as co-operators? Barbara Ehrenreich writes about this in *Blood Rites*, her theory of the origins of war. For Ehrenreich, our ancestors were those that somehow survived the nightmare of predation, 'when the terror of being ripped apart and devoured was never further away than the darkness beyond the campfire'. She finds throughout the world, in cultures as disparate as the USA and Japan, students reporting the same dreams of being eaten by predators. She explains that for decades our ego was so bloated that when archaeologists kept unearthing sites where big cat bones and human bones were intermingled, we assumed they were cats we had kept among us for ritual purposes. Rather than what they actually were: human remains in the stomachs of predators. Ehrenreich makes the point that the widespread belief in hunting as the 'exclusive factor driving human evolution' that was accepted in the first half of the twentieth century served patriarchal household norms and 'naturalised' the abusive status quo that women were to stay indoors and keep house, while men were to go out into the world and provide the bread. This allowed for a feeling of inevitability – that this was simply the way things were, and that there was no point in even dreaming of things being different.

In Ehrenreich's understanding of our origins, women would have had a vital part to play in the group's survival. Not relegated to the home, not the weaker sex, but necessarily tenacious and extremely strong. Protecting children at all times while moving through potentially hostile space. Fundamental in the gathering of food and in maintaining the vigilance and swift communication needed to stay alive, in preparation to flee or deter a potential predator.

Before we were the hunters, we were the hunted. And we learned to band together not to kill, but to preserve life, to escape predation.

In a 2014 study, healthy individuals were asked to watch videos of actors, people they did not know, plunging their hands into iced water. The physical temperature of the subjects' own hands dropped in response to these images. This is known as temperature contagion. It shows that in social interactions we physiologically respond to each other: when we see people who we are not related to and who we have no involvement with go through physical discomfort or shock, our bodies respond; the temperature of my skin drops when I see that you are cold. This response system facilitates 'emotional understanding and group coherence'.

We are empathetic beings who feel for each other. Our very success as a species is rooted in our ability to be aware of each other's needs, to notice each other's pain and to experience deeply felt physiological and emotional empathy.

Another study, published in 2017, found that while watching a piece of theatre, audience members' heartbeats synchronised. They responded 'in unison, with their pulses speeding up and slowing down at the same rate . . . Experiencing the live theatre performance was extraordinary enough to overcome group differences and produce a common physiological experience in the audience members.'

Beneath the surface we are connected.

/

Immersion in other people's stories cultivates empathy. When we are reading or listening to stories being told, provided there is enough tension in the narrative, our brains release cortisol into our blood to help us focus and concentrate, and also oxytocin, the chemical related to care and empathy. Theatre and music have long been arenas in which we examine our moralities and consider our shortcomings, as well as celebrate our virtues. Think of the tragic plays of ancient times. We watch the hero in denial of their weakness eventually fall because of their self-blindness. Think of the old folk songs, sagas of betrayal, pride, murder. Juicy morality tales, not unlike present-day TV dramas. All with lessons to teach about how best to approach the problem of living a life, that encourage us to greater compassion for those whose struggles we recognise. Stories and songs bring us into contact with our best and worst natures, they enable us to locate ourselves in other people's experience and they increase our compassion. But these things in a vacuum are useless. A story doesn't cultivate empathy just by virtue of its having been thought up; it must be engaged with to become powerful; the story must be read, the song must be listened to, in order to acquire its full charge.

/

Words on a page are incomplete. The poem, the novel or the non-fiction pamphlet are finished when they are taken up and engaged with. Connection is collaborative. For words to have meaning, they have to be read.

In the throes of creation that give life to text, the writer is the pilot of the force. They stand alone at the brink of an idea, trying to reel it in. But once the writer has delivered the work, it does not belong to them any more; it belongs instead to whoever picks it up and completes it. The writer's intentions for their own work are as misguided as a parent's intentions for the life of their child. What can you really know about what their life will become? After the conception and the safe passage to adulthood, your part in their future is reduced to backstory. They must become who they are, and this will be transitory because they will be new in whoever encounters them.

To really be useful to the connective power of the text, rather than interrogators, we must be the conductors. We, the readers or listeners, are crucial to the text, story or song becoming powerful. We are not impartial observers; we are a fundamental part of the circuitry; if we are not connected, the charge will not be able to flow.

The connective circuit is triangular. In order for a charged connection to be made and felt, there are three stations that must be fuelled with an equal power. These stations are writer, text and reader. You can substitute these terms depending on what form you are considering but the basic gist is that for the connection to happen, the creator of work, the work itself, and the person who will take that work on so that it will come to life need to be equally activated, conducting the energy, so the bulb can light up.

If we give as much as we expect to take from a novel, a poem, an image or an album (or a conversation, or a relationship), it has a greater chance of becoming profound. As readers, we feel this happen when something speaks directly to our experience and we feel the words burning themselves into us. We get some sense of the poet or the writer as someone we feel *knows* us. This is the circuit connecting. Like when I discovered the *Red Book* in Portland. You may forget the exact words, but you carry a relationship with the text through your life. You may think this was entirely because of the quality of the text, but it was also about the quality of your reading. It is the connection between the author, the text and you as you read, at a particular point, with a particular set of circumstances informing a particular emotional response, that created that sense of deep meaning.

As a poet who tours, I have been both the writer and the reader of my own work; and in committing my work to memory and going out each night to perform it, I have also in some ways been the text. I have felt the connection fire and misfire at all stages of this circuit.

Brand New Ancients was a seventy-five-minute-long poem that I told in theatres, scored for a quartet of drums and electronics, violin, cello and tuba. I wrote the poem over a period of many months, in week-long bursts of intense creativity, and once it was finished and on its feet touring, I saw first-hand that there were things Tempest-the-writer never knew about the writing that Tempest-the-reader discovered each night with increasing clarity. Themes emerged to me, the reader, once I had committed the text to my body and was delivering it to rooms of people. Patterns to the language that I hadn't been aware of when I was writing. Patterns between characters. I noticed links that helped me intuit meaning and remember the text, because they gave me a sense of why one passage led to another, but I have to say I was not aware of these links in the same way when I was writing. I have found this to be the case with every work I've toured since then. The reader undergoes a process of discovery that the writer side of myself is not involved in. This is why I made the decision to record my most recent album, *The Book of Traps and Lessons*, in one take, after committing it to memory. To try to get as close to that process of discovery as I could.

It wasn't only about the words themselves, but how the words spoken in sequence at the right depth of feeling became bridges between emotion and experience. Between audience and stage, between venue and crowd. Between the day that everyone in attendance had brought into the room with them, and the prospect of the night to come. When the connection is made, everything is linked and moving towards a moment of mutual feeling, a creative connection that binds the entire room into a unified present.

/

When I write characters, I am always trying to pull out the tension that exists between their interior lives – their small exchanges, private hopes and intimate relationships – and their exterior lives – the impossible largeness of the environment they exist in, and the day-to-day reality of what they have to do to get by. The characters often find it easier to spot depraved tendencies in the wider world than to face those same tendencies in themselves. Their arcs as characters are usually about coming to terms with the patterns of their own behaviour. Almost all of the characters in my various works are intent on facing a change. In trying to bring about a profound difference in their lives or relationships. For example, Harry, struggling to overcome her jealous insecurity in *The Bricks that Built the Houses*. Or the speaker 'I', desperate to learn how to love less co-dependently in *The Book of Traps and Lessons*. Or Bradley wondering how to reanimate himself and feel through his depersonalisation in *Let Them Eat Chaos*.

It is not only our immediate families and circumstances that affect our moralities, behaviours and life choices; the dominant narratives of the world at large are also pushing our decisions and desires. Think of the generational differences between what is acceptable now and what was acceptable then – from the loss of jobs-for-life to 'fame' becoming a viable career option in and of itself.

In my stories, many of my characters are prey to a pervasive numbness; it is pitched as the understandable toll of trying to make a living and a life. But an inability to notice one's own behaviour contributes to the apparent infallibility of the tropes of our day. If we can't even notice violence in ourselves, let alone root it out, how can we expect to dismantle it in the culture at large?

It is relatively easy to spot and damn the exploitation of a cruel boss against their workforce. Harder to spot and damn the same exploitation in your own household; is there one partner who shoulders an unfair share of the housework? Childcare? Financial responsibilities? The greed, malice, pride and treachery of the times can be seen everywhere else, in everyone else, exhibited clearly every night on TV for you to shake your head at, but can you spot it when you close the door at the end of the day, in the encounters that you yourself have with your loved ones?

I heard it best from Killer Mike and El-P: 'Lie. Cheat. Steal. Kill. Win. Win. Everybody's doing it.'

/

It is uncomfortable to learn new habits. Our old habits do not want to let go. I find myself switching off from conversations, getting distracted easily when other people are talking, or thinking of my own experiences when someone is trying to describe theirs. It's hard to notice because in a disconnected state, self-awareness is one of the first frequencies to be scooped out and muted. When this happens, I need creativity to reconnect me, even if it's the last thing I want; a creative connection brings a person closer to themselves when they have started to drift; this proximity is profound and encourages deeper focus and better listening, which in turn re-encourages profound connection.

A schoolgirl sits at her desk. Head on her textbook, staring at the pages. She is meant to be writing but she is restless and can't think straight. She begins to hit the table quietly, tapping out a beat with her fingertips, and she is lost momentarily in the pleasure of a rhythm.

A woman in her seventies is waiting at the bus stop, singing an old church song to pass the time. The much younger man waiting next to her closes his eyes so he can listen better.

A boy walks through the park at dusk, watching the birds skimming the tops of the branches.

A group of people act out a scenario of conflict in a theatre workshop and discuss how things could have turned out differently.

Can becoming a better or more engaged reader of text or listener to music really encourage me to become a better reader of and a better listener to other people, the world and myself?

I think so.

It's definitely helped me. Although I'm still shit at noticing my behaviour in the moment. I'm definitely better than I was before I knew to even notice that I wasn't noticing.

It's basically like this: anything that can remind me that at all times, other people are existing and that their existence is as fully felt as my own, is useful. Music and literature take me straight into someone else's experience, and straight out of my own.

Kabir says, 'Love does not happen with words.' If I'm to commit, I need to commit in action, not just in thought. A daily practice of intentionally connecting to someone else's story can offer me, the engaged reader, a lived example of how to approach an exchange without being exploitative, violent or selfish. But I can't cultivate this habit just from reading. At some point I need to take what I've been practicing out into the world, and start applying it to my encounters. Kabir also says, in the same poem, 'The love I talk of is not in the books. | Who has wanted it has it.' If I truly desire a more resonant experience then I will find it. It's already there.

Next time I'm about to cast a harsh judgement on a stranger who offends me, can I allow myself instead to see them as the flawed and complex human that they are? Full of heartbreak, loss, ambition and disappointment, walking a volatile path of all the things they've ever failed at? What about next time I'm about to judge my nearest and dearest harshly for hurting my feelings in one way or another? Can I do the same for them? Cast them as the protagonist in their own story, rather than as an accessory to mine?

Preparation

Damn braces: Bless relaxes.

WILLIAM BLAKE

There is something infuriating about writing this in the Covid-19 lockdown. Over the course of the last two or three months, 'connection' has become even more of a buzzword than it already was, useful mainly for encouraging downloads of conference apps. Just my luck to be stuck behind the zeitgeist. Look at it! Blocking the road. Here I am, idling, waiting for my ideas to flow freely instead of having to fight their way through the tight spaces left by the tank-like bulk of 'these unprecedented times'.

Online, you can't feel the surprising shift that I discussed at the outset of this book, the levelling of the room that happens after a performance. The internet makes it possible for like people to find each other, and this is extremely important. But it makes it difficult for unlike people to contact each other without their defences up. Anecdotally, growing up, all of my mates were heterosexual men. I had

61

to accept that my closest friends had no understanding of certain elements of my experience, and in fact I suppressed huge parts of myself so that my life could better reflect the experiences of my straight male friends. Online, I can find people who have similar experiences of gender and sexuality, and who have created spaces where my questions can find answers, where my experiences can feel common and valid. It is a relief to feel understood without having to point out the differences in lived experiences. But because of the importance of creating alternative communities, we have arrived in a place where we project selfhoods that are dependent on our differences. Communities develop in opposition to each other. The internet is increasingly a place to establish and reaffirm ourselves as members of this or that tribe, who share this or that belief system, and are suspicious of people who disagree. But as a 2015 study published in *Current Biology* found, 'The ability to express empathy – the capacity to share and feel another's emotions – is limited by the stress of being around strangers.'

The idea of a hostile band of 'others' just over that digital hill – The frothing crowds of woke vs unwoke, snowflake vs gammon, deep state conspiracy theorist vs mainstream news consumer or any other us-vs-themisms – adversely affects our abilities to empathise. Perceived threat makes us less trusting and open, further divorced from each other and clutching more fiercely to whatever it is that keeps us in community with whoever we have pledged our allegiance to.

We become vehicles for beliefs, for what we stand for or against. We mute our subtleties in order to project ourselves into the collective conscious as being entirely one thing or another, righteous and correct in our polarities. Glorying in the response this elicits from others. I am a Cross of St George or I am All Cops Are Bastards. And if you are offended then fuck you. I know who I am. I know what I stand for.

In *The Undiscovered Self*, Jung writes:

Most people confuse 'self-knowledge' with knowledge of their conscious ego personalities. Anyone who has any ego-consciousness at all takes it for granted that he knows himself. But the ego knows only its own contents, not the unconscious and its contents. People measure their self-knowledge by what the average person in their social environment knows of himself, but not by the real psychic facts which are for the most part hidden from them.

This is why poetry levels the room. Because it speaks to the psychic facts which are hidden.

To be judged by others is part of social life. We may tell ourselves that we don't care what others think of us but we evolved the ability to enjoy a good gossip in order to encourage certain traits and discourage others: selfishness was dangerous in prehistoric society, because if someone ate all the food then the others would starve. So, gossiping became a way of keeping a check on any undesirable behaviour. The difficult feelings that arise from transgressing social codes, from being 'talked about' by those you don't want to upset have been knitted into the fabric of our moralities for many hundreds of generations.

So how to gain better self-knowledge? How do I dig down beneath the painful strata of what people think of me, or what I think of myself because of what I think people think of me? What do I want to project? What do I actively seek to keep hidden? And anyway, what is the difference between self-knowledge and self-obsession? One encourages a defeat of the ego, the other encourages a feeding of the ego. One, a deeper experience of connection to ourselves, which enables a more nourishing connection to others. The other, disdain for the deeper needs of the self, which leads to disdain for others.

It is difficult to come to an awareness of your own needs and set boundaries so that you may protect yourself from your own transgression. It's easy to think loving someone, for example, means giving them everything you possibly can, ignoring your desires to better implement theirs, leaving nothing for yourself in the hope they'll do the same for you. The advert couples, the movie couples, the perfume couples, the TV portrayals of successful relationships are noxious. They find their way into the most surprising situations. Ever noticed yourself desperate to be rescued? Desperate to be the hero in the situation? Wanting to be loved at the expense of all else? Playing the femme fatale? The happy family? The handsome rebel? The jealous drunk? Nursing a screaming desire to be publicly acknowledged as 'the one'? Or to run off into the sunset with a new love and leave these suckers behind? Who are these people? Why have they stepped down out of those shitty adverts and turned up here at our kitchen tables affecting the way we say good morning?

'Know thyself' was the first of three celebrated maxims inscribed in the fore-temple at Delphi. Shakespeare tells us, 'To thine own self be true.' The disciples of the Egyptian goddess Isis believed they could contact the divine through self-realisation and that the kingdom of heaven was accessible through self-knowledge. Celebrated Golden-Era hip-hop artists, from the Wu-Tang Clan to Brand Nubian, from Rakim to Gangstarr, all make constant references to the importance of knowledge-of-self, drawing heavily from the tenets of the Five Percenters, an organisation and theological discipline born in Harlem, developed by an ex-member of the Nation of Islam, that teaches the fundamental significance of developing this knowledge as the first of its principles. And yet, we have arrived in the age of the self and, so far, as a culture, we have not been granted access to the divine. In fact, products for sale right now include a ring box that is also a mobile phone case, so that when you ask your beloved to marry you, the opening of the ring box brings up your mobile phone screen and starts filming your partner's reaction, perfect for sharing your special 'proposal moment' online. Have we misinterpreted the ancient wisdom? How can it be that in the age of self-care, self-harm

and self-improvement, knowledge of self hasn't
yielded the kingdom of heaven?

/

When life is the pursuit of status, and status is
measured in wealth, we grade the outcomes of our
existence by the possessions we accumulate or the
goals we can tick off our bucket lists. It's a poisonous
mythology, and even if we feel we don't subscribe
to it, our intentions need careful scrutiny to spot its
effects on our deepest drives. Why are we onstage?
Why are we pursuing our interests? Why are we hit-
ting the gym or the bar or the bookies? Why do we
want the partners we want? How are we able to tell
ourselves two truths simultaneously? Why are we
acting out our fantasies in secret? Why are we desperate for new clothes or expensive jewellery or a
different body? Why are we saving up money for a
deposit on a home of our own or a BMX or a BMW
or a face tattoo? Why is any of this acceptable to us?
We know, rationally, that a person's worth does not
equate to how adept they are at playing the imag-
inary game we were all born into. But when a person is not adept at this game, they fall short. They

become losers, relegated to the bottom rung of a ladder that hangs over nowhere. And their bottomness enables those on the next rung to get more purchase as they climb. And as we climb we begin to think we earned our lead. We accept that in any game, some people have to lose. Conveniently forgetting that life pushes out of all of us with equal ferocity and that the entire game is rigged.

So much is done to gain the respect of others. From childhood, into adolescence and on into maturity. We are crippled with doubt when we receive the disapproval of our peers.

We want to prove ourselves. Rather than look inwards, and confront the lack there, we push outwards, adorn ourselves with the trappings of the day or whatever gets us through the night. For me, the creative path began with the need for recognition, the credit of my peers. And then it was a record deal. And then it was money – I wanted to live off my art. And then it was accolades – I wanted to be praised. Why? What good does it do me when I am sat with the truth of me? Where does any of that get me if I can't bear my own company, can't relax in my own skin, can't see my own beauty and in fact am desperate to destroy myself?

68

In my characters, this is the pull to despair. The unacknowledged depths are what drive people to acts of callousness. It is why people can enact terrors in the name of profit. It is why people can commit to lives they cannot stomach. It is why people can function for years while keeping adulterous secrets. This non-acknowledgement of the full spectrum of a person's interior life by that person themselves makes it much easier to mute the parts that are inconvenient. And we build it into our readings of others. We hate for people to be as complex and multi-dimensional as they truly are. We like to keep people bracketed, neatly organised into arbitrary classifications of how *they* relate to *us*.

If you allow approval to define you, you will have no choice but to allow disapproval to define you when it comes. If you can be swayed by other people's opinions, if you are desperate for other people's acceptance, if you crave a position to boost yourself above your insecurities, deep creative connection will remind you that none of these things define you and actually none of this stuff is important. If you need approval to bolster your conviction, it is not conviction, it's an affectation. And it will melt away under the faintest scrutiny.

Approval and disapproval are not abstract ideas any more. They are visible, traceable currents that flow online, where everything we post solicits response. It is perversely easy to estimate our global rating; what is my worth as a human being? All these comments and likes will tell me.

How can I trust what anybody else stands for if I don't know what I myself am about? It's true that if people generally approve of what I'm saying, it is easier to believe that what I'm saying has worth. But when they stop approving, where will that leave me? Unable to ascertain whether or not what I have to say has any validity? I have to get a sense of my motives beyond the blinkered duality of approval or disapproval. It doesn't define me. I was born fallible and I'll die fallible, just like everyone else, no matter how much goes right or wrong in my life.

Problem is, I left my creative compass to rust while I navigated life by other people's standards, and now, when I really need it, it's stuck and I don't know which way to go.

I must know myself outside of what I produce, because who I am has got nothing to do with what I am capable of generating, what I fail at or what I achieve. Everybody fails. Life itself is failure:

eventually, it ends. That doesn't make it any less powerful. The focus on what I can successfully generate, on what I can monetize, on what I can contribute, is a systemic imprint that enforces a production/consumption mentality and keeps me in the thrall of needing to work to consume to value myself. If I can produce goods or services that can be exploited in order to maximise profit, I am valuable. If I can't produce goods or services that can be exploited for profit, I remain un-valuable. If I am the primary carer for my children, I have to labour at home all day in order to keep the home functioning and the children safe and well. My working hours are hard and long. But this labour is unmonetised and cannot be exploited for profit so it's not valued in society. If I am the primary earner in the same household, if I am the one who goes out to work, my experiences are valuable because my earning power means I am able to consume; that's what makes me important; my desires are encouraged in order to be catered for, in order to be met. If I do not have a 'job', or if I live in a low-income household, my needs are not valued in the same way as if I have regular wages that afford me an expendable income, and am out in the world prepared to part with money for things I enjoy.

I may be making great efforts to have healthy relationships, I may maintain a good regime of self-care, I may be a great listener who enjoys the company of friends and cares deeply for others, I may be dedicated to environmental causes, or to practicing a martial art or facilitating community events, I may be a skilled herbalist, or great at organising my living space or fantastic at helping my loved ones make difficult decisions; but if I do not get paid, my skills have no public worth, because what can't be sold can't be bought.

When I was finally able to make poetry my full-time job, I remember the blast of satisfaction I felt when people asked me what I did for a living and I was able to reply, 'I write.' To which their response would inevitably be, 'Sure you do. And do you get paid for that?' And, finally, I could say, 'Yes, I do! I make my living off writing poems.' The shift in the tone of conversation was weirdly pleasurable. Suddenly it was like, 'Oh, Okay! You're a "real" artist. You're making money! Not just a stupid pretend artist who does it for the "love".' The thing is, I'd been a poet long before I ever dared to take myself for one. I'd been a poet long before it paid my rent. But when I could finally say to others that yes I was *living* off my art, it made me feel

72

legitimate. Because I judged myself by the spirit of these times, which is concerned with 'use and value'. Rather than being in communication with the spirit of the depths, which wants me to 'refind my soul', or retune my creative compass.

But how do I do that?

It starts by realising you don't have to be concerned with how you measure up to someone else's ideas about your output. And even more importantly, you don't have to be concerned with how you measure up to other people's successes.

Poetry is rife with snobbery. It is also open and constantly transforming. It is not the case, as it is sometimes imagined, that the 'page' world is full of snobs and the 'stage' world is open-minded; it is more the case, in my opinion, that great poets, no matter which form they work in, are more likely to be generous spirits, who are interested in people, whereas mediocre poets, in whatever form, are more likely to be snobbish and uptight – obsessed with the shortcomings of other people's output. A mediocre poet may well define themselves in opposition to another poet's lack of style or talent, rather than in opposition to their own lack of style or talent, which is the mark of a more interesting writer.

It's tempting to define talent comparatively, but you are not in competition with anyone but yourself. You are trying to be a better writer (or lover, or friend, or human) today than you were yesterday. Bettering anyone else is entirely without consequence. But how do you know you've done that? How can you tell if you've improved, if you are 'any good' without relying on the barometer of other people's acceptance, approval or recognition?

The creative compass is the instinct that drew you to your discipline in the first place, and when you are in connection with it, it will tell you everything you need to know about how you're doing with your work. It will guide you through difficult creative decisions and will help you distinguish between a motivation to act from a need for approval on one hand, and a genuine creative compulsion on the other. Sometimes, the creative compass, a wounded pride and a fragile ego feel similar. They all want you to prove yourself. How do you know which is compelling you? How do you 'refind your soul'? You learn by getting it wrong. Once you've gone miles down the wrong path and ended up in a creative dead end, you learn something about how it feels to have got ahead of yourself. It is extremely important to learn this way. Things will go wrong. You will make mistakes. You will end up doing things that don't feel entirely right. This is how you learn how to dig at your compulsions, and really feel where they're coming from. It's a process of sensory reanimation. You are learning a new sensibility. Or, maybe more aptly, remembering an old one. There's nothing wrong with writing to get the approval of your peers. There's nothing wrong with wanting to be a singer because you think singing is cool. There is something wrong with allowing yourself to be coerced into action because you haven't come to terms with what you yourself want or don't want from your creativity.

Bukowski says, 'For yourself | not for fame | not for money | you've got to keep chopping.'

It is not the case that if something is esteemed highly but you lack an education in it, then it is not for you. It does not matter whether it is popular or canonical. If you are moved by a rapper that you listen to on YouTube, it's really not a big deal. You shouldn't have to apologise for it in literary environments. The same is true if you love a classical poet.

It isn't the case that you need to approach lauded works on bended knee. The pool of influence you draw from does not have to meet the approval of an academy or an institution, or be bound by the parameters of a genre, sub-genre or 'movement'. Listen to everything. Read as much as you can. Try to stay present and connected with whatever you're engaging with when you're engaging with it. Even if you're not into it. Ask yourself, why not? What choices are being made that turn you off? What don't you like about the way they've recorded those drums? What don't you like about the way the perspective shifts from chapter to chapter? If you want to be a writer, you need to read writers. Contemporary, fallible writers that arouse your jealousies and disdain, not just all your dead heroes. Same with music. Same with absolutely anything. Want examples of how to live, or how not to live? Look up. They're everywhere.

There is no success in writing. There are only better degrees of failure. To write is to fail. An idea is a perfect thing. It comes to the writer in a breathless dream. The writer holds this idea in their mind, in their body; everything feeds it. They have spent their entire lifetime up until that point honing the skills to get this idea out of the ether and down through their useless hands, on to the page. But it will never be right. There is no way that a writer cannot injure that idea as they wrestle with it. By the time it has revealed itself to be finished, when the deadline can't be put off any longer, the exhausted writer has learned another lesson about their own restrictions that they promise themselves they will overcome next time. But next time comes, and they are faced with new restrictions, new limitations, new impossibilities.

'Finishing' work, is what gives the artist the humility necessary to begin again. Many, many people have ideas. But to go through the agony of finishing that idea, realising you are so ill-equipped that, despite your burning conviction, your deep creativity, your relentless practice and your natural talent, you have *still* failed. You made a good go of it. The thing is out there, another step towards meaning. Next time, maybe you'll do it better. Or maybe you'll never do it again.

This is the reality of an artist's existence, and is what gives the artist the awe and respectfulness that is the mark of a good one. Even consumed with purpose, convinced that what *they* have to say is going to be important for the *world*, even then, with all that noble fire to create, it is still a process of failing. A process of persevering despite the failures and raising a quiet pride in the ability to keep failing, and hopefully, as Beckett would have it, fail better.

The difference between an artist and someone who dreams of becoming an artist is finished work. The person with the great ideas that judges other people's output as inferior to what they themselves could produce, but has never actually committed themselves to producing anything in full; this is the fallacy of artistic endeavour. Everyone is so sure they can do it, apart from the people who actually do it, who despite knowing that they must, are more sure every time that they can't.

Or as Czesław Miłosz so brilliantly put it, 'I did not say what I should have. | I submitted fog and chaos to a distillation.'

Going Out There

You never know what is enough unless you know
what is more than enough.
WILLIAM BLAKE

It can be a grave experience, going out there. There's
a deafening moment as I walk out from behind the
rig and see the stage in front of me, when my whole
body is in extreme agitation, I am shrunk to a minute awareness of each pump of blood and oxygen.
My energy is concentrated in the centre of my palms
and pushing upwards from my solar plexus. I shake
my limbs to try to move the nerves, I breathe out
long sounds to vibrate my lips and throat, but the
moment is completely consuming. It lasts until I
have taken the mic from the stand, held it up to my
mouth and begun to speak.

In my formative years, going out onstage was
joyous, revelatory, empowering, and it still is those
things. But the longer I've spent doing it the closer I've come to understanding the seriousness of
it. Standing up tall in the face of a cavernous room
and delivering something about my truth to people

I don't know, who in many ways feel they know me and have arrived at the gathering with the high expectations that come with forking out money for a ticket, making the childcare arrangements, booking the night off work, crossing the town or the city or the country to attend; or with the low expectations of the people dragged along by partners or mates that can't really be bothered to be there and anyway don't know what to expect; or the suspended expectations of the critics, journalists and bloggers who are there to remain distant rather than partake in the proceedings. I feel all of that energy when I step out. It can be a formidable undertaking, to meet the room each night. Sometimes it's like tackling a giant slippery monster, and other times it's like letting a bird out of my chest and watching it fly up into the light. I never know which it's going to be.

In my early twenties I was doing three or four gigs a night, three or four nights a week and had grown used to grabbing rest where I could get it. I remember one gig at a small festival, me and my bandmates Archie Marsh and Ferry Lawrenson were sat on a little sofa at side-of-stage waiting for our turn to go up, and I had fallen fast asleep. The person on before us shouted us out, my bandmates shook me, said,

'Come on, we're up', I opened my eyes and that was it. I grabbed my beer and went up there to do it, no problems. The stage was an extension of that sofa. There was nothing to prepare for; it was natural. I could literally do it in my sleep. Many times I went straight from the stage and out through the crowd, ran to the Tube to cross town and get to the next gig. I'd arrive, get to the front of the queue, push through the crowd to the stage, couple more drinks, get up there, do it again. Many times the gear broke, things malfunctioned; I would have to improvise a show with whatever we had left at our disposal. I found myself playing the character of the tough and friendly Tempest who could face anything, and that character carried me through. It suited me fine; it was who I was offstage, too, at the time. But the point is, there wasn't really any offstage. Every day was about getting the words out, to whoever I could find to listen, and that reality was all-consuming. It became the entirety of my existence.

/

If we are to believe the moral panic – that all the world's a stage since the advent of social media self-exhibition and the universe-at-your-fingertips advances in tech – how do we prepare for it? We turn on the phone in the morning and that's it. We're onstage. Over the course of our day, if we see something beautiful, funny, particular to our online self, we snap it, compose it, post it up. Anything we think, feel, witness, imagine or partake in becomes ammunition for the next pithy tweet, political statement, glamorous image or sarcastic caption; all moments are incomplete until they have been digitised, made browsable, and it all just sits there, on our various profiles, performing.

But I have learnt that performance is a deep art. Something that is solemn, that is of the spirit as much as the body, of the depths as much as the times, and it is something the performers need to prepare for with intrinsic attention. Even when exhausted; the meditation, the stretches, the drinking of certain liquids, the taking of certain foods at certain times, the set-up, the sound check, the mutual preparations between bandmates and tech team. How can it not be taking its toll on us that we are performing so constantly without any preparation or recovery? Without any real acknowledgement that that is what's happening? There is no way on or off the stage. No privacy afterwards. No quiet dressing room to sit in and come back to yourself. No 'real' self to come back to. You are getting all the accelerated feelings of acceptance, approval, self-assurance, but none of the deeper-register feelings of purpose, of leaving the self entirely, feeling a creative force come through the body, the surrender, the service, the mutuality.

Around the same time that I was falling asleep at the side of the stage and running from gig to gig four nights a week, I learned a lesson about boundaries: I realised I had none. I was in ambition mode. I wanted to make it. I wanted to be somewhere other than where I was at. I didn't want to be working in schools and shops and watching other rappers making music on TV. I had jealousy and I had a thorny pride and I was full of despair really that things weren't going better. I was involved in a scene that I didn't love. I wanted to make music but I was trapped in spoken-word to make my rent, and, to be brutally honest, I found the whole scene embarrassing. I should say that there were a lot of nights I really enjoyed being a part of, and a lot of poets I met from that world who I cherish as friends and who inspired my writing, but I felt it was important

85

to include that sentiment (of finding the scene embarrassing) because it goes some way to giving a sense of the energy I exuded as I walked into places at the time: full of myself. I lacked humility. I would storm up, do the set, leave. On to the next place, same thing – do the set, get the money. Go. Drunk the whole time. There was no onstage or offstage. Every gathering of people was a potential audience: kids at the bus stop or outside the take-away; the queue to get into a rave; any people, anywhere. It was a selfish way of looking at the world. Exploiting every happening for my own gain. All situations were seen through the filter of how could I develop my practice, how could I get people to listen to my lyrics? I was living in the kill-or-be-killed narrative. Prey to the tropes of the time. Not examining my desires, but allowing myself to be led by them. It's like St Augustine said, 'I was foul to the core, yet I was pleased with my own condition and anxious to be pleasing in the eyes of men.'

I suffered a blow because I wasn't living with any awareness; I developed nodules on my vocal cords, which are like blisters that stop the folds of the cords meeting and restrict the sounds you can make with your voice. My voice struggled to come out, there were whole octaves I was shut out from. I had thought my voice was just husky and that it was nothing to worry about; a testament to the harsher life I was living at the time, of very little sleep and lots of drink and drugs and constant rapping, often without a mic in busy rooms. Or busking with a practice amp and a ropey mic cable; fighting to be heard above crowds or sound systems. But it got to the point where I couldn't speak. I went to the doctor and was referred to an ear, nose and throat specialist. She put a camera down my throat and showed me the blisters. I could suddenly see why I couldn't make sound, and it was terrifying. My voice was not only my livelihood, it was also how I asserted myself in a room. My pass. The one thing about me, as I saw it at the time, that made it okay for me to exist in public, considering all the things that I was – dyke, fat, bloke, unfemale, unmale, anxious, full of dysphoric shame and discomfort, painfully shy and simultaneously overbearing in social situations or around people I didn't know. My voice and my lyricism gave me an escape route from my body and from the way being trapped in that body made me act and feel. My voice was my ticket to existence. And I'd lost it. There was no guarantee that after

87

the surgery it would come back. And if it did there was no guarantee that it would sound like me. They clamped my mouth open with a brace and knocked me out with anaesthetic.

I was forced to silence. Forced to choose my words carefully, having to write down anything I wanted to say. I learned to sit in a room and listen to my friends and family without trying to think of funny or interesting things to contribute; I learned to sit and be silent with people. To listen until someone had finished expressing their thought entirely, and beyond that, until they would reveal themselves to me in ways they never had before. Those with greater wisdom than me have the skill and self-assurance to listen like this without needing to be forced, but I was obviously in need of humbling. And the universe provided.

After surgery on the vocal cords, you need three full weeks of total vocal rest for the scar tissue to heal. That means not even a cough, a sneeze or a loud exhalation. No *sound* can come out of your mouth. I was reduced to the corporeal. After a lifetime of trying to escape my body, trying to be more than my body, trying to excuse my body, needing to talk my way out of my body because it was the wrong body and it didn't look like other people's bodies, I was my body entirely.

I learned that when you have no way offstage, you will damage yourself. There are things that need to happen to prepare a person for that level of exhibition. Why am I up here? What do I want? What is it that I'm trying to do? These questions need to be thought about and answered. At the time, it was just what I did. I didn't stop and assess. I just wanted to be heard. I just needed to do it. But why? What were my motives then? The true art? The deep creativity? No. It wasn't that. It began at that, at sixteen, lost and needing guidance – I discovered my passion and it led me to beautiful experiences. But it had become something disengaging. Rapping my way through every encounter, party, night out, night in, I had allowed it to define who I took myself to be. I'm a rapper, I'm a lyricist, I'm a poet. I have these words and that makes it okay to be who I am. I was nothing beyond that. I was of the times, but not of the depths. I was creative. But not connected.

/

The stage is a constant in my mind. I can't help but compare all experiences to the experience of being up there, playing music. I suffer from depression, anxiety and panic disorder. Sometimes, really basic things are beyond me. If I'm down, I can't leave the house to go shopping for food. I can't get off the sofa to brush my teeth before bed. I can't go to bed. I can't get up. I can't go outside at all in case the neighbours see me. I can't allow myself to be seen. But I can't be inside because I'm suffocating or sinking into a hole. I have good people around me, a strong network of loved ones, but I can't call anyone because I can't speak.

A few months ago, out of nowhere, I had four panic attacks in a single day. It can be debilitating.

I tell myself, 'Come on, you know you can do *this*, because you've done *that*.' But the problem is, the experiences do not correlate. Just because I can walk out in front of a drunk crowd and tell poems, that doesn't make it any easier to relax in a social situation with people I haven't known since childhood, or to get on the Tube when my brain is being weird, or even just get my shit together enough to cook myself a meal.

Sometimes in my quieter moments, when I am

well and busy doing something everyday, like the housework, or walking the dog, or sitting on my arse watching detective shows on TV, it comes back to me – the sudden image of being up there, all those people, the curved ceilings of grand spaces, the wall of applause that falls on the stage at the end, the people meeting the pitch of the performance with their own noise, the blood rushing through the body when you know you got to the end at last. The joy of the whole team, back in the bus, rolling on to the next city, knowing we got a good one. But comparing one moment that doesn't feel entirely real, to another moment that feels even less real doesn't help me locate myself any more fully in the present tense. I can't get connected by remembering a past moment when I felt connected, or imagining a future one. I have to make peace with wherever I am at. Sometimes where I'm at is unpleasant, but it's not as unpleasant as desperately trying to pretend things are fine when they're not.

The rush of touring, the rush of writing plays and seeing them go live, fades in the new light of whatever needs to be done with a day: fighting with a deadline, editing something difficult, trying to make it happen right now for whatever it is I am supposed to finish. The stage is a constant, but also – until I walk out there, it could be it never happened at all.

/

When I write about the stage, I am referring to the physical stage, but I am also referring to the symbolic stages we walk out on to each day. The stage of our online presence but also the stages we step on to at work or at school or when we link up with mates. Who we allow or expect ourselves to be for others. Erving Goffman was an American sociologist who published the first dramaturgical analysis of social interaction; he put it that we all play the parts that are assigned to us by class, sex, social position, and that as we play, we enter into a contract with whoever we are playing for. Everyone involved in the exchange will make-believe that this is reality. Nobody interrupting the drama, everybody comfortable in their role in the exchange:

> When an individual plays a part he implicitly requests his observers to take seriously the impression that is fostered before them. They are asked to believe that the character they see

actually possesses the attributes he appears to possess, that the task he performs will have the consequences that are implicitly claimed for it, and that, in general, matters are what they appear to be.

It is only when the person is offstage, or backstage, that they can cease the performance of selfhood or status. But for many, once the performance is over, it is hard to know who is left. Backstage, alone, the performer struggles to find the energy necessary to enquire into the quality of their character; without any of the reassurance that comes from social acceptance or the bliss of cohesion, how do you know how to be?

All stages, whether physical or metaphorical, come with the same risk. You cannot let who you are onstage patch up the cracks in who you are offstage. It is not sustainable. You will break down. If you are a wreck, but you pull yourself together enough to get up there and do it, it will catch up with you. I was on Oxford Street after a panic attack, crouched down in a doorway unable to move. I had to find my composure because I had to go and do an interview on the radio. I managed it. The interview went fine.

I could not understand how it was possible that I could pull myself together for a work commitment, but not for my own sanity.

Social pressure is a hell of a thing.

The stage me ended up dragging the other me through a life they didn't want. Dosed up on booze, drugs, sex, food or whatever else I was using to tranquilise, the part of myself that I hoped would just come along for the ride turned on me eventually. Whether it's panic attacks, depression, breakdowns or insomnia. Essentially, it's down to self-respect. How can I respect myself enough to give myself the energy I usually reserve for the people I perform for? The people I have to impress?

All this to say: you can't hide it and you can't force it.

When I need connection the most, it eludes me. I find myself lost, doing stupid things, losing control of my emotions and slowing right down to a dead pace. Nothing but air and silence. Just when I think it's gone for ever, that's when it comes back on me. Out of nowhere. As if it never left. I feel myself caught up and taken and fully myself again. It's like it needs me to have no expectations. It demands a complete change of perspective. I can be lost for days, struggling to even hold the pen because my hands are made of soil, and then finally I'll give in, start watching a documentary about Manny Pacquiao through half-closed eyelids, and suddenly it explodes into the room and I feel it break across me. Sometimes when it comes on strong like that, after an absence of days or weeks, it makes me cry. I sit and write in tears. I don't know why. Nothing's wrong! It's like I've crested a hill that I've been climbing for ever, and I finally get to see the valley beyond.

Feeling It Happen

If the doors of perception were cleansed, every thing would appear to man as it is: infinite.
WILLIAM BLAKE

I can't summon connection down from the ether and expect it to land in my lap. But I can do everything in my power to create a welcoming environment for it when it does decide to show up. This is the same for self-awareness. I can't expect deep revelations about the content of my character – or my life's trajectory, or why I tend to do X when challenged by Y – to just pop by when I'm frying onions. I have to put in a great deal of work to notice my own behaviour and even more if I am hoping to transform it. It's a craft. The work that I do on myself may not be evident in my daily exchanges, but little by little, if I continue, I hope that my actions will reflect my changing mindset, and next time, I promise myself, I'll do things differently. Getting on top of my shortcomings is not immediate; it's endless. It takes constant application. And even after years of it, I might think I've cracked it until I find myself reflected through the lens of a relationship, and I realise I'm in exactly the same spot that I was in years before. Repeating the same mistakes. Apparently treading water this whole time.

Craft is the hard work. Connection the reward. When I am discussing creativity or creative connection, I am not talking about the nuts and bolts of craft or technique. Much of creative connection is subconscious. Craft is the opposite. A good craft is built on solid foundations, years of practice and experimentation that can be relied upon at all times to steer you through the creative process. Craft is the thing you develop while you're waiting for connection to show up. Whole weeks pass so quiet and slow, you don't know what's wrong with you and you pretend everything's normal and you get on with editing the manuscript or practicing in double-time, but in the quietest, lowest parts of your consciousness, you hear the voice saying, *It hasn't come today. I haven't felt it*, and it leaves you spongy. Waiting for a friend who doesn't call. Going through the motions, chipping away at it. Free writes, first-person monologues from the perspective of minor characters, sixty-four bars on the same half-rhyme. Keeping the muscles toned. But not enjoying the reps.

I can switch on craft, but it is never the case that

I walk out onstage and actively switch on connection. It happens or doesn't happen regardless of my intentions. Neither do I intentionally stand in an audience and tell myself I am going to connect with whatever I am there to witness and partake in, but sometimes it happens. I've *felt* connection countless times, but I don't create it. I don't know why sometimes I'm connected and other times I'm not. All I know is it's a collaborative, communal feeling that takes the whole room or none of us. It seems like it comes through me if I can get myself out of the way. But any interference will impede it. Trying to make it happen stops it in its tracks.

It's the same with the words. I have to get out of the way of them. I can't say them too dramatically because they are already so rich; if I enrich the language further in the way I speak, it will make them indigestible. Ideally, the higher the register of the language, the plainer the tone of voice should be. Otherwise it's overkill. But at the same time, I mustn't restrict it. I mustn't intentionally make it plain, because then I'm controlling it, and that stifles discovery and connection. Peter Brook put it this way: 'He is not really making the music, it is making him – if he is relaxed, open and attuned, then the invisible will take possession of him; through him, it will reach us.'

Even when I go out there knowing I want to keep my vocal energy on an even keel, it's so hard to remain level with all the adrenaline of a performance and the desire to reach a crowd. With all the imagining that they don't like it, that they're not into it, that even as they stand in front of me, sweet, open people, I see the worst that could happen, brace for the worst – with all this, it's hard not to get caught in the wind tunnel and zipped along until I've completely forgotten I was supposed to get out of the way and have ended up blocking the language completely, pushing against it with all of my might.

If you force it, it will not open. Trying to *make* it mean something kills the meaning. It should occur to you fresh in that moment. It's *through* you not *because* of you. Connection is the same. It's not about a furious effort to slow down. It's about getting out of the way and discovering the pace that was there all along.

In performance, the passage of time changes; the moments shrink right down to one word followed by the next, but also expand out to be experienced as hardly a moment at all. Some nights, I begin, and it's already the end. I barely have time to breathe and it's over. Other nights, the laborious closeness of the language puts every word in my way and the whole thing takes for ever to build. I have some landmarks in the set, moments where I know, *Okay, there's ten minutes left.* Markers that tell me I'm out of the woods. It's not like I'm wishing the show away, it just happens when you've been night after night into the same thing. You begin to recognise its shape and that makes it easier to pull it out of yourself each night.

My work can be dark. It blooms with dark shapes, and in large rooms those dark shapes can feel menacing from the stage. But in every set there is a moment when I meet the darkness with light, and that creates the galvanising rush that comes at the end of the performance or album or long poem. There needs to be both, for me anyway. I have tried to write the light and not include the dark; I have thought to myself that an album full of positivity must be a more useful prospect to offer the world than an album full of grief. But it just hasn't come out that way yet. Balance is the hopeful goal and a true reflection of life cannot be either/or. I must accept that some days, I will feel numb and shut out from my own experience and other days I will be wide open, full of sensation, joyous and calm. Without the low plunge of the circle, how could I get enough momentum to crest the high arc?

A beautiful moment in the *Traps and Lessons* tour is the set's closer, 'People's Faces'. It is usually the moment when the clouds lift. We look out at the faces as they look up at us and each night it's true that we see a lot of people wiping tears away. It grows unbelievably tender in the room. This shocking feeling of connectedness, in amongst all the anguish of my lyrics, a spark of hope, a falling away of electronic sound to an acoustic piano, a simple declaration of tender feeling after over an hour of complex rhythmic wrestling with themes and narratives drawn from the darkest well of my experience – the theatre of the whole thing is in the theatre falling away and us onstage becoming just two people on a stage playing simply, speaking simply, and the people out there, really there, all in this together, feeling something happening.

/

This has been written during the 2020 pandemic lockdown. The music and theatre industries have been pushing for new ways for people to experience the feeling of live art through tech. Most days I have had at least one conversation with a friend or colleague about when musicians might be able to go back on tour again and what gigs might look like if or when they are eventually permitted.

But there is a depth of honesty to the live exchange that a screen immediately defeats. The screens – the one in your hand as you watch and the one in the room that captures the performance – close doors between the writer, the work and the reader. What we are left with is something to watch, not something to be a part of. Screens work for film, cinema, television. But not for live performance.

During lockdown, when physical connection was so heavily policed, we began to crave what we had previously taken for granted. How often did it feel like a chore you couldn't face to keep to a social arrangement? When we are forced to go without something, we begin to notice what it truly is. When we have it all the time, we have no need to tune in to its qualities. The cliché is a cliché because it is true: you don't know what you've got till it's gone.

When I am numb, how can I make myself connected? I can't. But I can try to create an environment that is welcoming for connection if it should
turn up. Abstinence helps. Taking a full day's break
from my phone helps me rediscover the pace of my
own mind, which is useful for feeling in full possession of my senses. Fasting helps. Tasting food after
a day without helps me give due importance to the
everyday acts of living. Reminds me of how lucky I
am to eat a meal. Ritual fasting is important in every
culture and religion. Except here, in the secular
West, where we expect all the trappings of success
without any of the self-examination necessary for
understanding its costs and the responsibilities that
come along with it.

Solitude helps. All the things that we always knew
were good for the soul take on new relevance now,
when the soul is trapped in concrete and glass, weary
from overstimulation, and underwhelmed by every
encounter.

We have come so far.

We have grown so vast and entitled. The entire
ecosystem that sustains us is buckling under our
weight. Surely, something has got to give. And yes,
we die later in life than we used to. Modern-day

women get to work and wear trousers. It's not all bad. But sometimes I need something radical to snap me out of the lonely daze. Something ancient and more human than everything we've built to keep us safe and quiet and nice and routine; all the convenient distractions of goal-orientated life, the numbness that holds up the curtain, the covering that takes the edge off the violence of our distant and not so distant past. I need the roar of a sound system or the carved emotion of a Rodin sculpture or Kool FM tape packs while I pull up the carpet or chisel tiles off the wall. I need creativity. Sometimes we need to prepare ourselves for it. Clear a space. Light a candle. Sit in particular postures. Or maybe we need to get dressed up the way we like and go out into the night to dance. Sometimes we have to put ourselves at the mercy of a force more abundant than the daily grind and throw ourselves under its hooves.

My creativity enables me to access other worlds that exist parallel to this one. But even with those tools, sometimes the other worlds are inaccessible, the sound is down. And I am trapped in two dimensions. Flattened by routine and the desire to live a routine life. I crave what society tells me will complete me. I crave a femme for my butch, a house of our own, a union of two with children who resemble us, enough money to protect us from hardship. Despite the fact that this white-picket dream is a product of the popular imagination and is actually completely at odds with my core beliefs, I still feel myself crave it! I still try to force it out of myself. The unnatural fit of a life without community. Trying to be all things to my partner, stifling each other when we mean to embrace. Lives built on outdated concepts in cities rich from ill-gotten gains. Unrepented wrongdoings bouncing off the masonry everywhere.

And yet.

I play music and I am granted access to a freedom so resolute it leaves me shining head to toe. I emerge from the performance covered in a gluey light. Looking out at the crowd, I see reality at last. People really feeling things.

Music.
Live music.
Performance of lyrics.
The theatre of resistance. The theatre of love.

Passionate declarations. Tiny, heartfelt observations.

Precision. Focus. Dedication to a craft, to a practice, that reaches for more than an expression of individuality. Reaching beyond *the self is the self is the self is the look at my self, have you seen how unlike all other selves my self is?* More. Stand in a crowd and hear music. Sit in a chair and watch a body cross a space. Feel shaken to the core by something un-numb that lives in the depths of all transactions based on LOVE. The passionate declaration of, 'I have seen. I have heard. I have felt. And it's for you that I am moved to speak. To sing. To dance here this way. I want to express more than myself. I want to express something about US.' And for a moment the numbness is wrenched away from you, because they're singing my life up there! That's my despair, my hope is in those drums! And I exist as more than an agent of my own individualism. An avatar, competing.

Connection balances numbness. Connection is the first step towards any act of acknowledgement, accountability or responsibility. It offers, whether fleeting or long-lasting, a closeness to all others. It is jubilant. Ecstatic. Without fear. I am in a space surrounded by people and I see them and I feel them, and my experience is such that when I leave this theatre, this sweaty club, this backroom bar, this grand arena or this park bench where I read this borrowed book and take the train across town to return to wherever it is I sleep, I will be aware of every engineer that tends the railway track, every station attendant that sweeps the rubbish from the platform and blows the whistle for the closing doors. I will be aware of my own humanity. I will be aware of my own complicity. I will show tenderness and deference to the people that I encounter.

Life as we know it is entirely unreal, entirely inhuman. We have lost each other under this selfie-system of hyper-competition. Music is the great invigorator. Artists don't make their work to inspire your collusion, your submission or your consumption of their ideals. They serve a purpose that is higher. Bigger. Deeper. Which is why you feel higher, bigger, deeper as you connect with their output. Even as you buy their T-shirts and send them on their tours around the world. Even then, in that moment, the integrity of the intention sustains the inevitable involvement of the band that you love in the capitalist industrialisation of their creative endeavours. The performance continues to be a deep searching for connection. They partake in the system, but are not engulfed in its numbness. They remain vigorous as long as they remain connected to this search.

Of course, art is as various as experience and not all music wants connection. Not all theatre cares about you. Culture, in the main, is a bourgeois pursuit, a reaffirmation of a mannered existence that cements prejudice and justifies ignorance. And much music is the product of mass manufacture, cynically assembled. It wants nothing but your clicks. It actively seeks your numbness. But that's not the kind of art I am talking about here. So let us say no more about it because it's everywhere and it doesn't need any more of our attention than it already has.

There is great work being made all the time. Find it where you find it. If it moves you, give thanks for being open enough to be moved, give thanks for being able to shake before your favourite band. This is the start. Hold on to it.

/

A person cannot function in this world if they are entirely of the other. But a person will not function any better by being completely closed to it. If they are, suffocation is felt. A stifling of the senses. A perplexing lack. Life happens, but nothing has a deeper resonance. Except for the instinctive shock-back-to-feeling of childbirth or death, no action feels profound enough to root the person in an experience of life that feels purposeful. Without purpose, days become mega-bright, vacuous pictures of days. Or an endless procession of duties to serve. Things done because this is what's supposed to be done. Things enjoyed because this is what I'm supposed to enjoy. I like this, because I'm like this. I'll do this because it's what my family have always done and it's what's expected of me. All the while, the spirit of the depths is not consulted. Not engaged with. Not even greeted at all. So, perversely, we can be online, projecting a deeper self out into the world, while neglecting the parts that create deep selfhood. The same can be said of acquiring the trappings of a life well lived. Fancy car. Status symbols. An attractive partner. Multiple attractive partners. Lots of people knowing your name. The latest clothes. An impeccably clean house. Ensuring your kids know their times tables by heart. Caring for your mum every day. Being seen as a pillar of the community. Never missing church. Whatever it is that motivates you to satisfaction.

You don't have to be engaged in 'art' to feel empathy or access the depths. The universal depths can be accessed through art, and personally that is how I have come to know them, but it is not always the case that drawing or writing will take you into a deep connection. Art-making, like anything else, can feel disconnected, routine and numbing. So, how to switch focus? Jung conducted his nightly rituals with words and images. Georgie Yeats used trance and séance. Mike Tyson smoked DMT, a substance secreted in the venom of a toad native to the Sonoran desert and found his life entirely changed by what he describes as the death of his ego: 'I realised I was nothing.' He says of the experience, 'I was happy.'

There are many ways to access a more resonant place. It starts by acknowledging that everything is resonating. When an opera singer hits a particular note and shatters glass, they are amplifying the resonant frequency of that object. All objects have a frequency at which they resonate. Including you.

It is not the case that numbness needs to be defeated to activate creativity. Numbness and connection are shades of the same spectrum.

It is the case that I have been learning, my entire life, to place vast value on possessions, on social status, on public approval. I have to retrain myself if I am to learn to value the minute and gradual things. Small exchanges. Genuine intimacies.

But how do I retrain myself?

I could start by paying particular attention to things I don't usually notice. The place where two trees meet at the roots. The bricks in the wall that I walk past. The floral shapes in the cast-iron railings. The colour of things. The feelings in my own body. And then, I could try paying particular attention in times of great stress or crisis. Or when I feel myself drifting off, pulling away into fantasy rather than remaining absorbed in the moment. Facing boredom, rather than succumbing to the impulse to distract myself from it.

It's the pushing back, the pushing of 'our' norms back out into the society at large that creates counter-culture, that presents an opportunity for change.

Don't be too hard on yourself.

You can't be present all the time.

But the closer we focus on our experience, the greater the awareness of the experience will be, the greater the immersion, the greater the possibility for connection.

So

Put your phone down.

Listen to the birds.

Build a fire in a quiet place.

Pay attention to the details when you kiss your lover.

When you have a conversation with your neighbour about their health.

When you cross the road or feed the cat or buy tomatoes.

When you cremate a parent.

When things go fuzzy, switch focus.

But if you can't switch focus. Don't switch focus.

There's no must. No have to.

Only try to. Choose to.

Walk in the pissing rain without hunching your shoulders.

Pay attention to the details when you're being rushed to hospital, haemorrhaging blood after an abortion.

Breathe in a lungful of air and breathe it out slowly.

Pay attention to the details when you've been kicked out and have to sleep in the park.

When you're trying to get the kids out the door but they've hidden their shoes and you're late for school and one of them is covered in blue felt-tip.

When your aunty gets sick but you can't visit her in hospital because of Covid-19.

Pay attention to the details when you start a crowdfunder for top surgery.

When you're going numb, switch focus.

Pay attention to the details when you drive off in a huff and reverse straight into a pillar.

When you finally get a pay-rise.

When you are reminded of a dead friend by a smell you end up following halfway down the street.

Drive to the coast and stare at the sea.

Walk in the woods in the early morning.

Spend a full day with no distractions.

No one really cares about what you said or how you said it. They are all too busy agonising over what they said or how they said it. Even if they're online ripping the shit out of you for what you said or how you said it, it's really themselves they're angry at and besides, other people's opinions do not define you.

What defines you? The very moment that you find yourself in.

Let go.

Every shouted greeting, every stalling car, every siren, every screaming kid, dog, fox, radio. All that sound out there is life and people living. Not background sound. But close up. Front and centre. See all those windows in all those buildings? Look up. There's life in there. Put yourself away. Let go of yourself. Tune in to other people. To the movement in the branches, the sudden coming of rain or the patterns in the waves. To how those two lie on the grass. To how that one sits on the bench with their hands clasped, looking up. To how those three stand at the crossing, playing with each other's hair. To how that young one shifts the weight of those shopping bags and tries to keep up with their mother's strong legs. This is it. This is the thing. This is the beautiful thing.

Notes

The epigraphs are from William Blake, *The Marriage of Heaven and Hell*, in *Complete Poems* (London: Penguin, 1977).

7 *In the particular* Fintan O'Toole, 'Modern Ireland in 100 Artworks: 1922 – *Ulysses*, by James Joyce', *Irish Times* (24 Dec. 2014), https://www.irishtimes.com/culture/modern-ireland-in-100-artworks-1922-ulysses-by-james-joyce-1.2044029, accessed 1 July 2020.

19 *Life in that room* James Baldwin, *Giovanni's Room* (London: Penguin, 1956), p. 67.

27 *numinous beginning* C. G. Jung, *The Red Book: Liber Novus* (New York and London: WW Norton and Company, 2009), p. vii.

29 *the figure of serious mental illness* 'The Homeless Mentally Ill', *Harvard Health Publishing* (March 2014), https://www.health.harvard.edu/newsletter_article/The_homeless_mentally_ill, accessed 1 July 2020.

35 *Speak then of sick delusion* Jung, *Red Book*, p. 150.

38 *as a living* Jung, *Red Book*, p. 129.

39 *He whose desire* Jung, *Red Book*, p. 129.

45 *when the terror* Barbara Ehrenreich, *Blood Rites: Origins and History of the Passions of War* (London: Granta, 2011), p. 78.

46 *exclusive factor* Ehrenreich, p. 67.

47 *emotional understanding* Ella A. Cooper, John Garlick, Eric Featherstone, Valerie Voon, Tania Singer, Hugo D. Critchley, Neil A. Harrison. 'You Turn Me Cold: Evidence for Temperature Contagion', *Plos One* (31 Dec. 2014), p. 1, https://journals.plos.org/plosone/article?id=10.1371/journal.pone.0116126.

48 *in unison* 'Audience members' hearts beat together at the theatre' [press release], UCL Psychology and Language Sciences, 17 Nov. 2017, https://www.ucl.ac.uk/pals/news/2017/nov/audience-members-hearts-beat-together-theatre, accessed 27 May 2020.

48 *our brains release cortisol* Paul J. Zak, 'Why Your Brain Loves Good Storytelling', *Harvard Business Review* (28 Oct. 2014), https://hbr.

org/2014/10/why-your-brain-loves-good-story-telling, accessed 26 May 2020.

55 *Lie. Cheat. Steal.* Run the Jewels, 'Lie, Cheat, Steal', in *Run the Jewels 2*, [digital release] (New York: Mass Appeal, 2014).

57 *Love does not happen* *Kabir: Ecstatic Poems*, translated by Robert Bly, (Boston: Beacon Press, 2004), p. 52.

62 *The ability to express empathy* 'The Secret of Empathy: Stress from the Presence of Strangers Prevents Empathy, in both Mice and Humans', *Science Daily*, 15 Jan. 2015, https://www.sciencedaily.com/releases/2015/01/150115122005.htm, accessed 27 May 2020.

63 *Most people confuse* C. G. Jung, *The Undiscovered Self* (London: Routledge and Kegan Paul, 1958; repr. Abingdon: Routledge, 2002), pp. 3–4.

64 *selfishness was dangerous* Will Storr, *Selfie: How the West Became Self-obsessed* (London: Pan Macmillan, 2017), pp. 41, 52.

66 *Egyptian goddess Isis* Muata Ashby, *Mysteries of Isis: The Ancient Egyptian Philosophy of Self-Realisation* (Florida: Sema Institute, 1996), pp. 59–60.

66 *The Five Percenters* Shawn Setaro, *The Five Percenters Dominated Rap's Golden Age: Can They Return to Prominence?* Retrieved from Complex: https://www.complex.com/music/2018/11/five-percenters-dominated-raps-golden-age-can-they-return-to-prominence, 13 November 2018.

66 *proposal moment* 'Meet the Smartphone Case That Doubles as a Ring Box and Delivers the Ultimate Proposal Selfie', The Jeweler Blog (15 Nov. 2017), https://thejewelerblog.wordpress. com/2017/11/15/meet-the-smartphone-case-that-doubles-as-a-ring-box-and-delivers-the-ultimate-proposal-selfie/, accessed 27 May 2020.

75 *for yourself* Charles Bukowski, 'the creative act', in *The Last Night of the Earth Poems* (New York: HarperCollins, 1992), p. 204.

78 *I did not say* Czesław Miłosz, 'Gathering Apricots', in *Provinces: Poems 1987–1991*, translated by Czesław Miłosz and Robert Haas (New York: Carcanet, 1991), p. 557.

86 *I was foul* St Augustine, *Confessions*, translated by R. S. Pine-Coffin (London: Penguin, 1961), p. 12.

92 *When an individual* Erving Goffman, *The Presentation of Self in Everyday Life* (New York and London: Penguin, 1956; repr. 1975), p. 28.

101 *He is not really* Peter Brook, *The Empty Space* (London: Penguin, 1968), p. 47.

113 *Georgie Yeats* Emily Ludolph, 'W. B. Yeats' Live-in "Spirit Medium"', *Jstor Daily* (5 Dec. 2018), https://daily.jstor.org/wb-yeats-live-in-spirit-medium/, accessed 27 May 2020.

113 *I realised I was nothing* Dan Le Batard, 'The Spiritual Awakening of Mike Tyson', *ESPN Boxing* [video] (11 May 2019), https://www.espn.co.uk/video/clip/_/id/26701682, accessed 27 May 2020.

Acknowledgements

With thanks to my editor Alexa von Hirschberg and my agent Rebecca Thomas for trusting my writing. Without you two there would be no book at all.

Thanks also to Dan Carey and Ian Rickson, for your guidance and encouragement.

The very deepest gratitude to my friends: Jim, Maisie, Luce, G, Mica, Munna, Stef, Lisa, to my sisters Laura, Sita, Ruth and Claudia, my brothers Jack, Matty and Joel, my nieces and nephews Bess, Ziggy, Archie, Poppy and Ernie and my beautiful parents Nigel and Gilly, for always having my back, for looking after me when I wasn't well, for being around even when I myself was not. With so much Love.

And lastly, my thanks to you, the engaged Reader, for connecting the circuit.